HAL•LEONARD

JAZZ PLAY-ALONG®

Book & Audio for B♭, E♭, C and Bass Clef Instruments

volume 2

MILES DAVIS

10 MILES DAVIS CLASSICS

T0040768

Arranged and Produced by Mark Taylor

PLAYBACK+
Speed • Pitch • Balance • Loop

To access audio, visit:
www.halleonard.com/mylibrary

6567-5018-6399-5961

ISBN 978-0-634-03916-4

HAL•LEONARD®

Visit Hal Leonard Online at
www.halleonard.com

World headquarters, contact:
Hal Leonard
7777 West Bluemound Road
Milwaukee, WI 53213
Email: info@halleonard.com

In Europe, contact:
Hal Leonard Europe Limited
1 Red Place
London, W1K 6PL
Email: info@halleonardeurope.com

In Australia, contact:
Hal Leonard Australia Pty. Ltd.
4 Lentara Court
Cheltenham, Victoria, 3192 Australia
Email: info@halleonard.com.au

Visit Hal Leonard Online at **www.halleonard.com**

Explore the entire family of Hal Leonard products and resources

 SheetMusicPlus

Miles Davis

Arranged and Produced by
Mark Taylor

Featured Players:

Graham Breedlove-Trumpet
Tony Nalker-Piano
Jim Roberts-Bass
Steve Fidyk-Drums

HOW TO USE THE AUDIO:

Each song has two tracks:

1) Split Track/Demonstration

Woodwind, Brass, Keyboard, and Mallet Players can use this track as a learning tool for melody style and inflection.

Bass Players can learn and perform with this track – remove the recorded bass track by turning down the volume on the LEFT channel.

Keyboard and **Guitar Players** can learn and perform with this track – remove the recorded piano part by turning down the volume on the RIGHT channel.

2) Backing Track

Soloists or **groups** can learn and perform with this accompaniment track with the RHYTHM SECTION only.

ALL BLUES

C VERSION

BY MILES DAVIS

BLUE IN GREEN

C VERSION

BY MILES DAVIS

FOUR

C VERSION

BY MILES DAVIS

HALF NELSON

C VERSION

BY MILES DAVIS

MILESTONES

NARDIS

C VERSION

BY MILES DAVIS

SEVEN STEPS TO HEAVEN

C VERSION

BY MILES DAVIS AND VICTOR FELDMAN

SO WHAT

C VERSION

BY MILES DAVIS

SOLAR

C VERSION

BY MILES DAVIS

TUNE UP

C VERSION

BY MILES DAVIS

ALL BLUES

Bb VERSION

BY MILES DAVIS

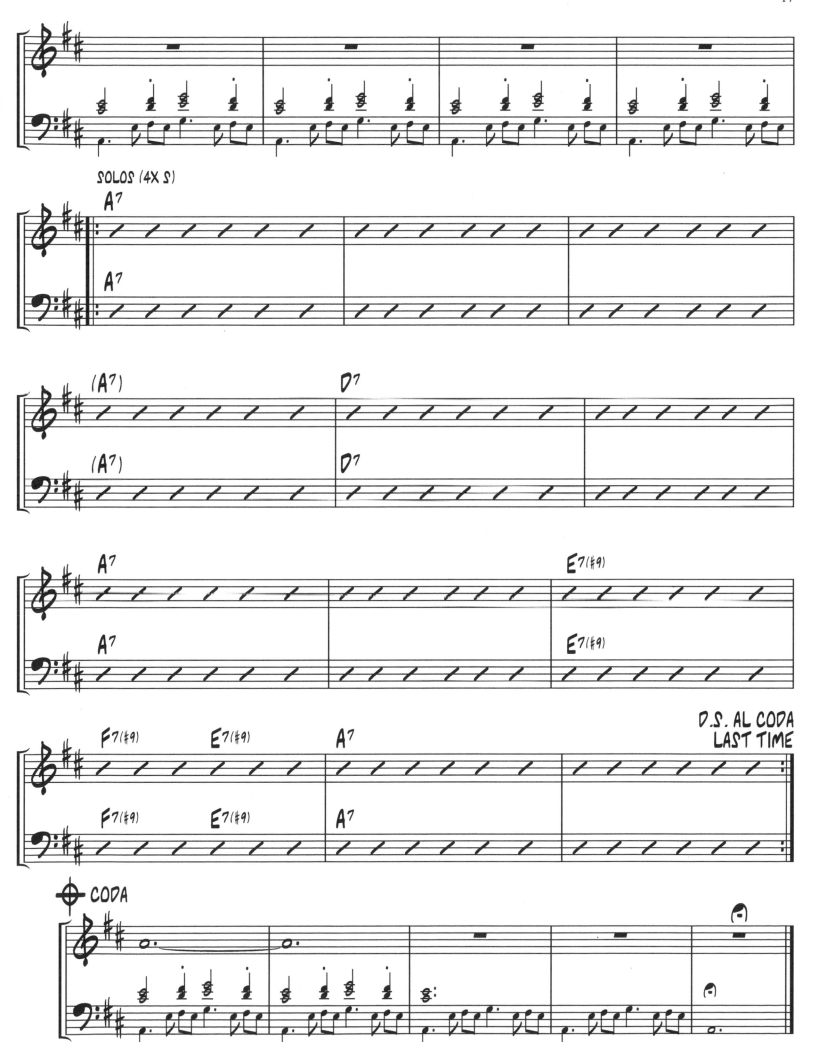

BLUE IN GREEN

Bb Version

BY MILES DAVIS

FOUR

HALF NELSON

MILESTONES

Bb Version
BY MILES DAVIS

NARDIS

Bb VERSION

BY MILES DAVIS

SEVEN STEPS TO HEAVEN

Bb Version FAST SWING

BY MILES DAVIS AND VICTOR FELDMAN

SO WHAT

Bb VERSION

BY MILES DAVIS

TO CODA

* SOLOS
Emi⁷

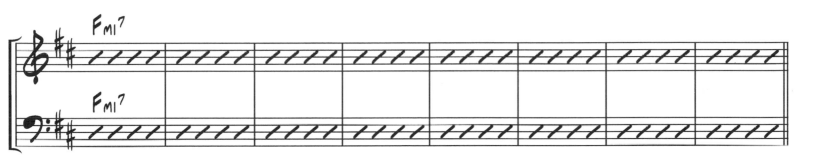

Fmi⁷

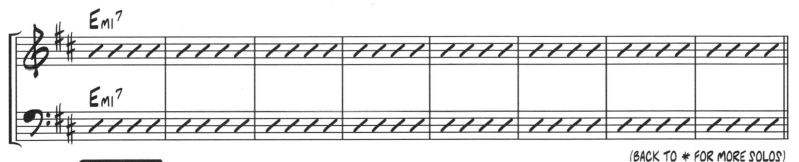

Emi⁷

(BACK TO * FOR MORE SOLOS)

(AFTER SOLOS)
(PIANO)

D.S. AL CODA   CODA

SOLAR

Bb VERSION

BY MILES DAVIS

TUNE UP

Bb Version

BY MILES DAVIS

ALL BLUES

Eb Version

BY MILES DAVIS

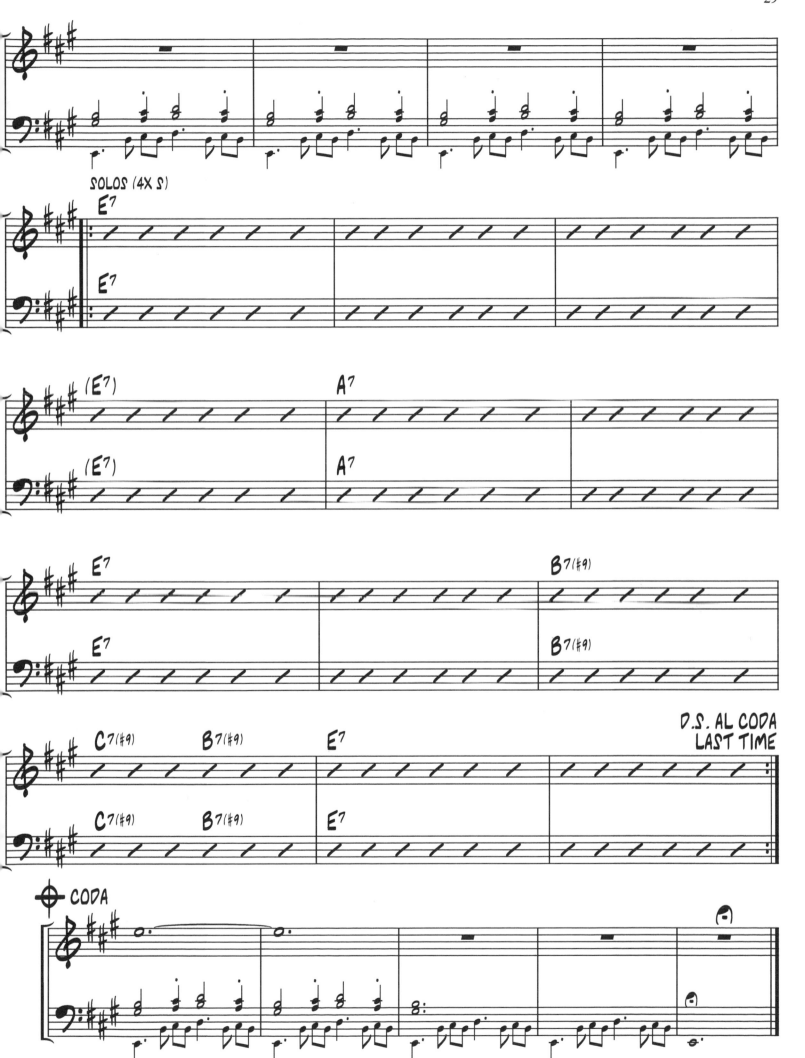

BLUE IN GREEN

Eb VERSION

BY MILES DAVIS

FOUR

Eb VERSION

BY MILES DAVIS

(BACK TO ✳ 2 MORE TIMES FOR SOLOS)

HALF NELSON

Eb Version

BY MILES DAVIS

MILESTONES

Eb Version

BY MILES DAVIS

NARDIS

Eᵇ Version

BY MILES DAVIS

SEVEN STEPS TO HEAVEN

Eb Version

By MILES DAVIS AND VICTOR FELDMAN

SO WHAT

Eb VERSION

BY MILES DAVIS

SOLAR

Eb VERSION

BY MILES DAVIS

TUNE UP

Eb VERSION

BY MILES DAVIS

ALL BLUES

BLUE IN GREEN

FOUR

BY MILES DAVIS

HALF NELSON

MILESTONES

BY MILES DAVIS

NARDIS

BY MILES DAVIS

Seven Steps to Heaven

BY MILES DAVIS AND VICTOR FELDMAN

SO WHAT

9: C VERSION

BY MILES DAVIS

SOLAR

𝄢 C VERSION

BY MILES DAVIS

TUNE UP

JAZZ PLAY-ALONG SERIES

For use with all B-flat, E-flat, Bass Clef and C instruments, the **Jazz Play-Along Series** is the ultimate learning tool for all jazz musicians. With musician-friendly lead sheets, melody cues, and other split-track choices on the included audio, these first-of-a-kind packages help you master improvisation while playing some of the greatest tunes of all time.

FOR STUDY, each tune includes a split track with: melody cue with proper style and inflection • professional rhythm tracks • choruses for soloing • removable bass part • removable piano part.

FOR PERFORMANCE, each tune also has: an additional full stereo accompaniment track (no melody) • additional choruses for soloing.

To see full descriptions of all the books in the series, visit: